A MOUNTAIN
FOOD CHAIN

A MOUNTAIN FOOD CHAIN

ODYSSEYS

A. D. TARBOX

CREATIVE EDUCATION•CREATIVE PAPERBACKS

Published by Creative Education and Creative Paperbacks
P.O. Box 227, Mankato, Minnesota 56002
Creative Education and Creative Paperbacks
are imprints of The Creative Company
www.thecreativecompany.us

Design and production by Blue Design
Art direction by Rita Marshall
Printed in the United States of America

Photographs by Alamy (Blickwinkel, Jack Thomas, Sven
Zacek), Corbis (Charles Krebs), Getty Images (Altrendo
Nature, Tom Brakefield, Frank Cezus, China Photos, Tui De Roy,
Jim and Jamie Dutcher, Jack Dykinga, Tim Fitzharris, Daisy
Gilardini, Chris Johns, Taylor S. Kennedy, Steve Lewis, David
McNew, Tom Murphy, David Ponton, Richard Price, Michael S.
Quinton/National Geographic, Norbert Rosing, Ron & Patty
Thomas, Michael Townsend, Joseph Van Os, Ian Waldie,
Konrad Wothe, Winfried Wisniewski)

Copyright © 2016 Creative Education, Creative Paperbacks
International copyright reserved in all countries. No part of
this book may be reproduced in any form without written
permission from the publisher.

Library of Congress Cataloging-in-Publication Data
Tarbox, A. D. (Angelique D.)
A mountain food chain / A. D. Tarbox.
p. cm. — (Odysseys in nature)
Summary: A look at a common food chain in the Rocky
Mountains, introducing the ponderosa pine tree that starts the
chain, the mountain lion that sits atop the chain, and various
animals in between.
Includes bibliographical references and index.
ISBN 978-1-60818-540-5 (hardcover)
ISBN 978-1-62832-141-8 (pbk)
1. Mountain ecology—Rocky Mountains—Juvenile literature. 2.
Mountain ecology—Himalaya Mountains—Juvenile literature. 3.
Food chains (Ecology)—Rocky Mountains—Juvenile literature.
4. Food chains (Ecology)—Himalaya Mountains—Juvenile
literature. 5. Rocky Mountains—Juvenile literature. 6. Himalaya
Mountains—Juvenile literature. I. Title.

QH541.5.M65T37 2015
577.5'3—dc23   2014038228

CCSS: RI.8.1, 2, 3, 4; RI.9-10.1, 2, 3, 4; RI.11-12.1, 2, 3, 4

First Edition HC 9 8 7 6 5 4 3 2 1
First Edition PBK 9 8 7 6 5 4 3 2 1

Cover & pages 4–5: A great horned owl
Page 2: The Rocky Mountains, Colorado, U.S.A.
Page 6: A ponderosa pine in winter

CONTENTS

Introduction 9

Ponderosa Pine: Majestic Mountain Tree 12

Magnificent Mountain Bird 16

Mountain Pine Beetle: Battle in the Bark 23

Himalayan Hunter 25

High-Mountain Herbivore 31

Three-Toed Woodpecker: Beetle Hunter 37

World's Largest Flier 41

Marten: Tree Stalker 50

Mountain Lion: King of the Mountain 63

Bamboo Bear 75

Selected Bibliography 76

Glossary 77

Index 80

Introduction

Abird swoops through the sky. In the depths of the sea, a whale dives. A wolf runs for miles across a snow-covered plain. They fly, swim, and travel in search of food. Animals spend most of their time looking for a plant or animal to eat, which will nourish them, provide energy, or help their offspring survive. A food chain shows what living things in an area eat. Plants, called producers, are the first link

OPPOSITE: While the bald eagle rules the skies of upper North America, the closely related while-tailed eagle (pictured) does the same in much of northern Europe and Asia.

on a food chain. Consumers, or animals that eat plants or other animals, make up the other links. The higher an animal is on the food chain, the less energy it receives from eating the animal below it. This is why there are more plants than plant eaters, and even fewer top consumers. Most animals eat more than one kind of plant or animal. Food webs show all of the possible food chains within a wildlife community.

ountains are tall, majestic rocks that rise from the land like ladders to the sky, and they

can be found on every continent. Formed by volcanoes or by the folding and raising of Earth's crust, mountains are unique natural environments because several different biomes can be located on, or at the base of, a single mountainside. About 50 million to 100 million years ago, the North American Rocky Mountains were formed by plate tectonics. Twenty-five million years ago, magma erupted through volcanoes, raising the peaks of these mountains to enormous heights. Despite the cool temperatures and low oxygen levels found at higher elevations, many plants and animals live in the Rocky Mountains. These plants and animals make up numerous food chains, including one that begins with a pine tree and ends with a big cat.

Ponderosa Pine: Majestic Mountain Tree

In 1540, Spanish explorer Francisco Vasquez de Coronado marched into the Rocky Mountains with his small army. He was searching for gold but did not find it. Instead, he encountered a wealth of natural treasures: the unique animals and plants of the Rockies. The Rocky Mountains are considered the backbone of North America and run 3,000 miles (4,828 km) from Canada to New Mexico. The heights of the mountains vary from 4,920 feet (1,500 m) up to the tallest peak, the 14,433-foot (4,399 m) Mount Elbert in Colorado. Water drains from the Rocky Mountains to rivers, such as the Columbia and Rio Grande, which eventually flow to the Gulf of Mexico and the Atlantic and Pacific Oceans.

Weather in the Rocky Mountains can be unpredictable. In the summer, the morning may begin warm and sunny, but the afternoon may bring gray skies and a snowstorm. Temperatures can also be quite different from the base of a mountain to the top of it. For every 1,000 feet (305 m) of elevation increase, the temperature drops 3.5 °F (1.9 °C), and the difference between the north and south side of a mountain can be as much as 82 °F (45.6 °C) due to the amount of sunlight received

OPPOSITE Ponderosa pine trees tend to grow taller at lower elevations, such as around lakes in foothills. Scientists classify the pines into four slightly different subspecies.

and the shadows cast.

Temperature and moisture affect which plants will grow on a mountain, as well as on which side and at what elevation they will grow. The top of most mountains is similar to a cold desert, with almost no life. However, lower on the mountain, slopes are often blanketed by green forest. Trees such as whitebark pines, which produce seeds that are an important food source for grizzly bears, grow at elevations as high as 11,500 feet (3,505 m) in the Rocky Mountains. Ponderosa pine is the predominant tree found at the montane, south-facing elevations, at 5,500 to 9,000 feet (1,676–2,743 m). On some stretches of mountain slopes, ponderosa pine is the only tree species for thousands of acres. However, ponderosas have not always grown where they are found in the Rocky Mountains today.

Magnificent Mountain Bird

Swooping from the sky at 150 miles (241 km) per hour, the golden eagle can see a rabbit as far as a mile (1.6 km) away. With vision eight times better than that of a human, golden eagles search their territory for rodents, rabbits, and birds to eat. Females are larger than males, measuring up to 3 feet (91.4 cm) in height and weighing up to 15 pounds (6.8 kg). Making their nest of sticks and leaves on top of a mountain or in tall trees, golden eagles mate for life and return to the same nest every year, adding to it each time. Eagle nests can sometimes extend as long and wide as a car. Golden eagles are protected in the United States. Before 1963, thousands of the big predatory birds were poisoned or shot by ranchers fearing for their livestock. Now, it is against the law to even own a golden eagle feather, with punishments of jail time and fines of up to $10,000. American Indians are the only citizens exempt from this rule because of their religion and traditions.

Radiocarbon dating has revealed that 50,000 years ago, other trees lived where ponderosas now thrive. At that time, the mountains were about 41 °F (22.8 °C) cooler than they are today. Because of warmer winter temperatures today, ponderosa pine trees can grow higher in the mountains. Another factor in ponderosa pines' modern abundance is their fire-resistant nature. More than 60 percent of a ponderosa pine must be burned before it will die. Most forest trees cannot survive fire, so when the ground is dry and lightning strikes, ponderosa pines may be the last trees standing.

Reaching heights of up to 160 feet (48.8 m), some ponderosas can be as wide as 8 feet (2.4 m). The trees can also be long-lived, reaching 1,000 years or more in age. The needles on ponderosa pines are evergreen and can grow as long as a sheet of paper. Among the needles, small brown seeds develop inside cones. The ponderosa seeds are collected and eaten by squirrels and bears. If the ponderosa seeds do get a chance to germinate in the mountain soil, most will not survive past the first few years because seeds and young trees require a lot of water over several years in order to develop roots. As an adaptation to survive drought, ponderosas develop deep taproots, which sometimes go into the ground as far as 36 feet (11 m). They also develop lateral roots, which can extend as long as a basketball court, to absorb water

OPPOSITE Mountain-elevation lakes are often ringed with trees that thrive at high altitudes and are known for water that is exceptionally cold, calm, and clear.

from rain and snowmelt. This double-duty root system not only helps the trees get the moisture they need, but it also makes them sturdy and stable, even in strong winds.

n July 1805, famous American pioneers Meriwether Lewis and William Clark came across ponderosa pine trees that were missing their bark as they traveled through the Rocky Mountains. When the two explorers first saw the ponderosa pines, they were unknown trees to them, but not to Sacagawea, a Shoshone woman and wife of a French translator who was traveling with Lewis and Clark as a guide. She explained that hungry American Indians sometimes ate the inner bark of the trees (as did animals such as black bears). Later, five large ponderosa trees were cut down, and five canoes were made. Ponderosa pine canoes carried Lewis and Clark and their party over rivers for a large portion of their trip to the Pacific. Wood from ponderosa pines is still used by humans today to build furniture, canoes, and houses, and small ponderosas are sometimes used as Christmas trees. Many animals, including black bears, porcupines, and squirrels, depend on ponderosas for food or shelter. Ponderosa trees also attract small but serious predators capable of killing not only a single tree but an entire forest.

Mountain Pine Beetle: Battle in the Bark

There is an ongoing war being waged in the mountains. The mountain pine beetle may be a small insect, only about one-third of an inch (7.6 mm) long, but it is armed with the perfect weapons to attack trees. Using its six clawed legs and a mouth that moves like a pair of scissors, the mountain pine beetle easily cuts through bark.

Instead of bones, the beetle has an exoskeleton, or hard outer shell, that protects it and gives it shape. Tiny hairs called setae cover its exoskeleton and help it to hear and to feel objects. Nerve cells make up the mountain pine beetle's brain, and a nerve cord runs the length of its body, controlling the insect's flying, walking, and other motor skills. On the beetle's head are sense organs called antennae, which are used for hearing, smelling, and tasting. Its compound eyes work like dozens of pictures displayed on a television screen, making it possible for the insect to detect motion. The beetle has two pairs of wings located on its thorax, or the middle section of its body, but it does not use both pairs for flying. Called elytra, the outer wings are hard and protect the flying wings underneath as the beetle crawls inside a tree. In the beetle's abdomen are holes

Himalayan Hunter

With thick, spotted, white-and-black fur, snow leopards are well suited for the cold climate of the Himalayan Mountains in Asia. Snow leopards are about the same size as the North American mountain lion, but their coloring, choice of prey, and abundance are all quite different. Snow leopards are endangered because of poaching, or illegal hunting, for their pelt and bones, which are sought after for use in certain Asian medicines. Their numbers are also low because ranchers often kill the leopards for taking livestock. Snow leopards are able to kill prey two times their weight, but their favorite prey are long-horned mountain sheep called bharal. They like to attack bharal from a rock, leaping down on unsuspecting sheep traveling along the mountain. After killing a bharal or other large herbivore, snow leopards sometimes take up to four days to eat it. Snow leopards will stay near their kill, eating and resting, chasing away vultures and other **scavengers**, until they have finished. If large prey cannot be found, snow leopards will eat large rodents called marmots.

BELOW Despite their small size (about the length of a popcorn kernel), hungry mountain pine beetles can kill even the biggest ponderosa pine by attacking in great numbers.

that allow it to breathe and a heart that pumps blood around its inner organs.

Mountain pine beetles use pine trees for food, shelter, and nesting sites for their young. It is the female mountain pine beetle that searches for a new tree, usually one of good width (10 inches, or 25.4 cm, or so) and around 80 years old. Using her powerful jaws, she bores into the bark like a drill until reaching the phloem, or inner bark. She makes a J- or S-shaped tunnel in the wood and digs rooms that will hold her future eggs.

From inside the tree, she sends out scent signals called pheromones to other pine beetles in the area.

ountain pine beetle pheromones act as a chemical language. The beetle might give off a phero- mone that tells other beetles to join her in the tree. Or she might give off a pheromone that tells other beetles that her tree is full. Mountain pine beetles communicate through sound as well as through pheromones. Using its wing to rub a special part of its abdomen, a beetle trans- mits sounds humans cannot hear to deliver a message to

other beetles. In this way, a female beetle might announce that she needs a mate, or that she has found one.

After mating, female mountain pine beetles lay as many as 80 white eggs—each one slightly larger than the period at the end of this sentence—in the tree. Two weeks later, the eggs hatch into larvae. Pale and wormlike, with a tiny, brown head, the larvae feed on the tree and make horizontal galleries all the way around it. As the larvae grow, they eventually stop feeding on the tree and enter their next phase, called the pupal stage. The larvae make pupae chambers and then rest.

During this resting phase, the beetle's internal organs shift to the position they will be in as an adult, and the pupae undergo metamorphosis, a process that can take two weeks to a month. After the beetles emerge from their pupae chambers as adults, the whole cycle begins again as the new beetles bore through the other side of the bark and fly off into the forest, looking for a new tree.

The ponderosa pine does have some defenses against mountain pine beetles, and sometimes the tree is successful in defeating its tiny adversaries. When pine beetles bore into a tree, often they become caught in the tree's sticky pitch, die, and get pushed out of the holes they made. To avoid this, pine beetles coordinate an attack on a tree. With many beetles attacking the pine tree at the same time, some will make it through to set up galleries, mate,

High-Mountain Herbivore

When people first see a pika, usually at mountain elevations of 8,000 to 13,000 feet (2,438–3,962 m) in Europe, Asia, or North America, they usually think it is a guinea pig or some other kind of rodent. Pikas are actually more closely related to rabbits, and like them, they are herbivores. Pikas eat thistles, fireweed, and grasses, and they take extra vegetation back to their plant stack. Like rabbits, pikas will eat their own dung in order to get all vitamins available from their food. Pikas do not hibernate, so they use their stored plants for food during the winter. Often, pikas can be seen on a rock lying very still. They sun themselves daily, even in the winter, to warm up and to keep an eye on their territory. Pikas can bleat like a goat, bark, and even sing. When a predator—such as a golden eagle or marten—is spotted by pikas, they become very vocal to alert their pika neighbors.

and lay their eggs, even while others get caught and die in the tree's pitch.

ountain pine beetles also counter a tree's pitch by carrying the blue stain fungus in their mouth. The beetles and fungus have a symbiotic relationship. As the beetles bore through the bark, the fungus grows and spreads, blocking the tree's pitch and thus preventing the tree from killing and pushing out the beetles. In this way, both the beetles and the fungus benefit. With lots of pine beetles underneath the bark, the tree is soon overwhelmed

and usually dies within one or two years. There are patches of forest in the Rocky Mountains that appear the color of dried blood, the end result of trees losing the battles beneath their bark. Feeding and living beneath the bark of pine trees helps protect mountain pine beetles from the mountains' cold temperatures and blustery wind. However, hard bark will not come between a certain feathered tree-tapper and its desire for plump beetles.

Ponderosa pine trees grow along the Pacific coast and in the southwestern deserts of the U.S., but they can dominate mountain vistas like no other tree species.

Three-Toed Woodpecker: Beetle Hunter

The forest echoes with the sounds of tapping. High on a ponderosa pine tree trunk, a three-toed woodpecker clings to the bark. Over and over, it strikes the tree with its beak, like a fist pounding at a door. Most woodpeckers have four toes, but this stout little woodpecker has no problem gripping the sides of trees with only three. The bird's size—about

OPPOSITE: Three-toed woodpecker parents make frequent trips to and from their nests to feed their young. Consuming mostly beetles, the young can fly after just three weeks.

the length of an adult's hand—and its white-colored back make it easy to identify. Female and male three-toed woodpeckers look alike, except the male looks as if he is wearing a small, yellow hat.

A three-toed woodpecker's light weight of 2.3 ounces (65.2 g) allows it to nimbly swoop up and down from tree to tree, and its long, powerful claws and short legs help it firmly hug the tree's bark. Almost the length of its head, its long, pointy bill is strong like a hammer.

TAKEAWAY

Female and male three-toed woodpeckers look alike, except the male looks as if he is wearing a small, yellow hat.

Its tail feathers are as stiff as cardboard, which helps it anchor itself in position to feed on moth larvae or to peck out a home.

When three-toed wood-peckers are ready to mate, they pick out a dead or live pine tree for their nest. Using their beaks, they drill a hole large enough to get in and out of and hollow out a cavity inside. They may line their nests with a few wood chips. The female lays three to six eggs in May or June, and both parents take turns incubating them. After two weeks, the young birds hatch, and the parents take turns feeding the newborns. The young woodpeckers stay in the nest for about 24 days, and then they are ready to fly.

The parents watch over the young as they try out their wings and claws for the first time. A few days later, the young leave the nest area and start their own lives in the mountain forest. When they are around two years old, they will find a mate and select a tree in which to make a nest and raise their young. If it is lucky, a three-toed woodpecker will live to be six years old.

World's Largest Flier

Found in the Andes Mountains of South America, the Andean condor is the largest flying bird on Earth. With a wingspan of 10 feet (3 m) and a standing height of 4 feet (1.2 m), its presence in the sky or perched on a mountain cliff is impressive. Weighing 30 pounds (13.6 kg) and possessing a sharp beak and powerful talons, it resembles an eagle in build. Yet the condor prefers to eat carrion—animals, such as llamas, that are already dead. Flying as far as 200 miles (322 km) a day, condors usually search for food as a flock. They do not fight over dead carcasses but follow a hierarchy as to who will eat first. The oldest condor is considered the most dominant and feeds first, followed by the rest of the males, and finally the females. Bacteria break down the remnants the condors leave behind, putting nutrients back into the soil that help mountain plants such as polylepis trees grow. Many South American villagers think condor organs cure sickness; even the bird's eyes are roasted and eaten to improve eyesight. The Andean condor is today an endangered species due to overhunting.

Hunched posture, wing spreading, and vocal rattling are also aggressive displays these birds use toward perceived threats.

Three-toed woodpeckers show aggressive behavior toward other woodpeckers and animals they feel are too close to their nest. Lowering their head and pointing, they may use their bill like a sword to strike intruders such as squirrels. Hunched posture, wing spreading, and vocal rattling are also aggressive displays these birds use toward perceived threats. The yellow feathered cap on a male three-toed woodpecker raises up when he feels threatened. He may swing his head, too.

Most birds prefer to perch atop tree branches, but three-toed woodpeckers are most often seen clutching the sides of tree trunks. Usually they look for food alone, but sometimes pairs of them can be seen on the same tree. They do not migrate but sometimes fly to warmer, lower mountain elevations during the winter.

A three-toed woodpecker's territory may cover three-fifths of a square mile (1.6 sq km). The bird has been known to fly even farther away to feed at other locations on the mountain, especially during a mountain beetle outbreak. The three-toed woodpecker is very important in controlling mountain pine beetle

The three-toed woodpecker is a busy but quiet part of the mountain food chain. It barely makes a peep as it pecks away at tree bark and probes holes for insects.

populations, as a single woodpecker can eat thousands of the damaging beetles a year. Some scientists believe global warming is making it possible for mountain pine beetles to strike trees at increasingly higher altitudes, where the colder temperatures used to prevent them from going. There are about 830,000 three-toed woodpeckers in North America and Eurasia, but they are increasingly vulnerable. Due to logging operations, woodpeckers in the mountains and elsewhere are losing their habitat. At present, when there is a pine beetle epidemic, there are usually not enough of their natural enemies, such as woodpeckers, to control them.

A three-toed woodpecker hunts for mountain pine beetles by first locating a snag, a tree recently killed by pine beetles. Grasping the trunk of the tree with its claws, the woodpecker uses its strong beak to tap and chip away at the bark until the outside layer is removed. With short breaks for rest, the woodpecker stays on the tree for long periods of time as it drills for beetles, devouring the plump young larvae and crushing the hard exoskeletons of the adults it finds. The mountain pine beetle and its larvae can do nothing to stop the three-toed woodpecker from coming into their home and can no more escape its attack than the ponderosa pine tree can escape the mountain pine beetles. Within seconds, the beetles become part of the mountain food chain. However, even while feeding, the woodpecker needs to think of its own safety as well as that of its young, as there is a predator in the trees searching for birds to eat.

High-elevation lakes play a role in the mountain food web. These remote lakes often hold trout, which are a valuable food source for such hunters as eagles and bears.

Marten: Tree Stalker

Often seen running along tree branches with the balance of a tightrope walker, the American marten is sometimes called the pine marten because of its arboreal, or tree-living, lifestyle. The marten is a medium-sized member of the weasel family, about 25 inches (63.5 cm) long. A male marten is slightly larger than a female, and its tail makes up

A marten is at home in the trees as well as on the ground and is also an excellent swimmer.

most of its length. It weighs about three pounds (1.4 kg), and its thick, soft, reddish-brown fur keeps it hidden as it climbs and runs along the bark. In the winter, hair grows between the animal's toes, so it is able to stay warm as it runs on the snow.

When a marten stands on all fours, it is only about six inches (15.2 cm) in height. Often, a marten will stand on two feet like a bear to have a better look around. Always careful to avoid predators such as the great horned owl, a marten runs in a zigzag pattern with lots of jumps when hunting on the ground for voles and pikas. A marten is at home in the trees as well as on the ground and is also

OPPOSITE Although American martens are sometimes called pine martens, the true pine marten (pictured) is a separate species found in wooded regions of northern Europe.

an excellent swimmer. Unless raising young, a marten usually lives alone.

Martens are found in Alaska, throughout Canada, and across the Rocky Mountains. When early European settlers came to America, martens were plentiful in the Southeast, but because of habitat loss, they are no longer found there. Martens can live 15 years and usually start having offspring when they are around 2 years old. In July or August, females start scent marking to alert males that they are ready to breed.

TAKEAWAY

Martens do not hibernate and can be found hunting both day and night. They tend to be most active right after dawn ...

The males become very aggressive and fight with one another during this time. After the female mates, perhaps with more than one male, the martens go their separate ways. The female will raise the young by herself.

A female marten has delayed gestation, which means that her pregnancy does not begin right away. The active part of her pregnancy is only 27 days, but the female may not give birth for up to 9 months after mating. To make her den, she takes over a former woodpecker nest or makes a new nest in a hollow tree and lines it with leaves. As many as four baby martens, called kits, are born in March or April. When the kits are around five weeks old, their mother starts to feed them meat from squirrels, voles, or birds.

Seven weeks after giving birth, when her kits no longer need her milk, the mother leaves, and her young are forced to fend for themselves. Martens do not hibernate and can be found hunting both day and night. They tend to be most active right after dawn, when many prey animals, such as birds and squirrels, are moving about. They can also be found stalking the trees or ground for food around sunset. Martens are territorial creatures.

Martens are naturally inquisitive and playful. The little animals, which have been raised successfully as pets, often hunt by investigating holes in tree trunks.

A male's territory may be up to three square miles (7.8 sq km), while a female might claim up to one square mile (2.6 sq km). Martens scent-mark around their ground territory and in the trees they visit. If a male finds another male in his area, there will be a fight. However, male martens will allow several females to be in their territory. Martens communicate with each other by making sounds that resemble chuckles or screams.

The mountain forest is normally a serene place, but it can suddenly erupt with frenzied bird cries, alerting other birds that a marten is near. Stalking the limbs and trunks of trees, the marten looks for woodpecker holes. Using its keen senses, the marten listens for the hungry cries of young birds, such as three-toed woodpeckers, begging to be fed.

nce a three-toed woodpecker nest has been located, the marten ignores the squawks of the mother woodpecker and possibly even the stabs of her bill as it scurries past, trying to squeeze its head into her den. Adult woodpeckers are hard to catch, but their young are

not. The marten snatches one of the young woodpeckers in its jaws, breaks its neck, and carries it down the tree to a hiding place, perhaps under a fallen log.

An opportunistic hunter, the marten is pleased when it finds an easy kill such as baby birds. It will return over and over again to the woodpecker nest to try to take the remaining woodpecker young and the adults, if it is able. The dead three-toed woodpeckers that the marten does not immediately eat are cached, or stored in a hidden place, for leaner times. Although martens rely on their speed and teeth to snatch birds such as woodpeckers, there is another opportunistic hunter in the mountains whose speed and teeth are much more fearsome.

Mountain Lion: King of the Mountain

At nine feet (2.7 m) long from nose to tail and standing as tall as a dinner table, the mountain lion is the largest wild cat in the U.S. and Canada. With 2-inch (5.1 cm) fangs and dagger-like claws, the mountain lion is built to hunt and can weigh well over 200 pounds (90.7 kg). The mountain lion goes by several names, including puma, cougar, and panther. Early explorers called it *gato monte*, Spanish

OPPOSITE: As notorious predators, mountain lions have superior eyesight and speed but often prowl after their prey, waiting for the right moment to attack.

Because of overhunting, mountain lions are extinct from eastern North America and are endangered, or at risk of extinction, in other areas.

for "cat of the mountain," which is how it got its most common name.

The mountain lion's coat is a shade of light brown, helping it blend into its environment. The lion's ability to retract its claws into its large paws helps it keep its nails sharp. It also allows the mountain lion to walk silently and sneak up on prey animals such as white-tailed deer. Its hind legs are bigger than its front legs, giving it the ability to jump to great heights (as high as 18 feet, or 5.5 m) or leap long distances.

Since the first Europeans came to America in the 1600s, humans have persecuted the mountain lion, mostly out of fear that it would eat their livestock. Because of overhunting, mountain lions are extinct from eastern North America and are endangered, or at risk of extinction, in other areas. The animal's range today is limited to the western half of North America and the Rocky Mountains.

n a mountain lion habitat, there might be 4 lions in a 62-square-mile (161 sq km) area, with 1 male for every 2 females. Females have a 90-day pregnancy and give birth to one to 6 cubs under cover such as thick brush or a pile of rocks. The father of the cubs does not help raise them and may even later kill them if he comes

OPPOSITE A mountain lion's preferred prey is larger deer, and it travels an average of six miles (9.7 km) per nightly hunt, alternately stalking, waiting in ambush, and resting.

across them in his territory. A mountain lion mother nurses her cubs until they are two to three months old. She will teach them how to hunt, and after the cubs are about two years old, they will leave her and go off to find their own hunting territories.

Mountain lions prefer to stay close to rocks and brush for cover and usually avoid open areas. Hunting mostly at night, they spend the day resting on a rock ledge. They sleep close to their kill if the animal, such as a bighorn sheep, is too large for them to devour all at once. Mountain lions are usually quiet animals, but when they do make noise, it sounds a bit like a human whistling, and females sometimes make loud yowls in their attempts to call for males when they are ready to breed. Both males and females growl as well.

Because they spend most of their time alone, territory is important to mountain lions, and they may fight to the

A grown mountain lion has little to fear from any other predator except humans, but young cubs stay close to their mother for protection from bears and male lions.

death over it. The big cats mark their hunting areas with scrapes, which are piles of leaves, rocks, and dirt pushed together, often near trees. They urinate and deposit feces on top of the scrapes to complete the territory marking.

In order for an adult mountain lion to stay healthy, it must eat the equivalent of a 100-pound (45.4 kg) deer every 10 days. It often takes a week for a mountain lion to thoroughly hunt its territory. Because of its high calorie

TAKEAWAY

In order for an adult mountain lion to stay healthy, it must eat the equivalent of a 100-pound (45.4 kg) deer every 10 days.

needs, the lion is an opportunistic hunter and will eat the tiniest of prey all the way up to animals weighing six times as much as itself. It prefers to eat hoofed animals such as mule deer. However, a marten, although much smaller than a big herbivore, is at least a snack for a hungry mountain lion.

A mountain lion can climb trees, but it prefers to do most of its hunting on the ground. While the marten is on the ground searching for small prey, such as voles, it may be spotted by a prowling mountain lion. The mountain lion stalks toward the marten slowly and silently. It tries to get within 20 feet (6.1 m) before attacking. In one great pounce, the mountain lion crushes the marten's bones and neck. Carrying the dead marten in its mouth, the mountain lion takes it to a more secluded spot to eat it or gives it to its cubs. Using the same methods it uses to kill a 3-pound (1.4 kg) marten, the mountain lion can take down an 800-pound (363 kg) elk.

The marten in the mountain lion's belly is linked to the three-toed woodpecker, mountain pine beetle, and ponderosa pine tree in the mountain food chain. After the mountain lion dies, perhaps from disease or from a fight with a rival lion, its body will be devoured by scavengers and further broken down by fungus. Once the mountain lion's body has returned to the soil, plants such as the ponderosa pine tree will grow in the nutrient-rich dirt left behind, and the mountain food chain will begin again.

BELOW The great leaping ability of mountain lions is well documented. This skill is frequently put to use, both for navigating rocky terrain and for launching surprise attacks.

Bamboo Bear

The digestive organs of giant pandas are like those of a carnivore—short and unable to break down all of the material in plants. Yet these bears, found in the Qinling Mountains and other temperate mountains of China, are plant eaters. Ninety-nine percent of their diet is a plant called bamboo, and they must eat up to 40 pounds (18.1 kg) of it each day. It takes between 10 and 16 hours for pandas to eat all this bamboo. When pandas are not eating, they are sleeping. Giant pandas are endangered, with only about 1,600 left in the world. Poaching is partly responsible for the low panda numbers. The Chinese government imposes strict punishments—including imprisonment for life—for the killing of pandas, but the crime still happens. Panda populations are also declining because of the bears' need for bamboo. Different bamboo plants flower and die in 10- to 100-year life cycles, and pandas migrate all over the mountain to get enough food. With China's human population at more than one billion, the human need for roads, farmland, and housing continues to infringe on the pandas' need for habitat.

Selected Bibliography

Alsop, Fred J. III. *Smithsonian Handbooks: Birds of North America*. New York: DK, 2001.

Bolgiano, Chris. *Mountain Lion: An Unnatural History of Pumas and People*. Mechanicsburg, Penn.: Stackpole Books, 1995.

Leeson, Tom, and Pat Leeson. *Panda*. Woodbridge, Conn.: Blackbirch Press, 2000.

Lyttle, Richard B. *Birds of North America*. New York: Gallery Books, 1983.

Wilson, Don E., and Sue Ruff, eds. *The Smithsonian Book of North American Mammals*. Washington, D.C.: Smithsonian Institution, 1999.

Woodward, Susan L. *Biomes of Earth: Terrestrial, Aquatic, and Human-dominated*. Westport, Conn.: Greenwood Press, 2003.

Glossary

adaptation	a change an animal species makes over time—such as growing thicker fur or eating other foods—to survive in its environment
bacteria	microscopic, single-celled organisms that can live in the soil or water or inside animals and plants; some bacteria are helpful to their host, but others are harmful
biomes	regions of the world that are differentiated from others by their predominant plant life and climate
evergreen	trees and shrubs whose leaves, needles, or branches stay green throughout the year
fungus	a classification of organisms that do not have chlorophyll (the green coloring of plants) or inside supporting tissues; examples include mushrooms and molds
germinate	to begin to grow and sprout from the ground
incubating	sitting on eggs so that the warmth will help the young inside develop until they are ready to hatch
habitat	the place a plant or animal lives
larvae	the early stage of growth for some animals such as insects; the young animal often does not look like it will as an adult

metamorphosis	a process in which the shape of an animal undergoes dramatic change
migrate	to move from one climate or location to another to find food or to breed
montane	a region of a mountain in which large evergreens are the predominant life form
nutrients	minerals, vitamins, and other substances that provide an organism with what it needs to live, grow, and flourish
pitch	a sticky combination of moisture and nutrients that a tree makes and normally releases toward the top of its branches
plate tectonics	a theory that explains how the movement of Earth's crust is responsible for the position of the continents, mountain building, volcanic activity, and other geological processes
predators	animals that live by killing for their food
radiocarbon dating	a method of determining the age of an ancient object by measuring the amount of carbon 14 (radioactive atoms) inside it
scavengers	animals that feed on animals found dead
scent marking	a form of animal communication—usually done with urine, feces, or special glands—that informs other animals about territory boundaries or other information

species   animals that have similar characteristics and are able to mate with each other

symbiotic   a relationship in which two different organisms live together and receive benefits from each other

temperate   characterized by a moderate temperature, without lengthy periods of hot or cold

territorial   describing animals that have an attachment to a property and mark the boundaries of it, usually with feces and urine, and often will fight to keep it

Index

Andean condors 41
bacteria 41
bamboo 75
bears 14, 19, 22, 75
bharal 25
bighorn sheep 66
fungus 32, 72
giant pandas 75
global warming 46
golden eagles 16, 31
great horned owls 51
marmots 25
martens 31, 50–52, 54–55, 59, 60–61,
    71, 72
    communication 59
    dens 54
    habitat range 52
    kits 54–55
    life span 52
    prey 51, 55, 60–61, 71
    reproduction 52, 54
    size 50–51
    territories 59
mountain lions 25, 63–66, 70–72
    cubs 65–66, 72
    habitat range 65
    names 63–64
    persecution 64–65
    prey 64, 66, 70, 71–72
    reproduction 65, 66
    size 63
    territories 65, 66, 70, 71
    vocal sounds 66
mountain pine beetles 23–24, 27–30,
    32–33, 43, 46, 47, 72
    attacks on pine trees 23, 27, 29, 30,
        32–33, 46
    communication 28–29
    eggs 27, 29, 32
    larvae 29, 47
    metamorphosis 29
    pheromones 28
    reproduction 29
    size 23

mountains 11, 13, 14, 18, 46
    formation 11
    heights 13, 14
    locations 11, 13
    temperatures 11, 13, 14, 18, 46
nutrients 41, 72
pikas 31, 51
ponderosa pine trees 14, 18–19, 21, 22, 27,
        28, 29, 30, 32–33, 37, 38, 46–47, 72
    bark 21, 22, 27, 30, 32, 33, 37, 38, 47
    defense against beetles 30, 32
    fire resistance 18
    human uses 22
    life span 19
    roots 19, 21
    size 19
snow leopards 25
squirrels 19, 22, 42, 55
three-toed woodpeckers 37–40, 42–43,
        46–47, 54, 60–61, 72
    bills 37, 38, 39, 42, 47, 60
    defensive displays 42
    eggs 39
    habitat loss 46
    life span 42
    nests 39, 40, 42, 54, 60, 61
    prey 46
    reproduction 39–40
    size 37–38
    territories 43
voles 51, 55, 71
white-tailed deer 64

BOOK CHARGING CARD

Accession No. _____ Call No. _____

Author _____

Title _____

Date	Borrower's Name	Date Returned